F O R : _____

Millions of spiritual creatures walk the earth unseen, both when
we wake and when we sleep: All these with ceaseless praise his
works behold both day and night.

J O H N   M I L T O N

F R O M : _____

Requests for information should be addressed to:
Inspirio, The gift group of Zondervan
Grand Rapids, Michigan 49530
http://www.inspiriogifts.com

Compiler: Rebecca Currington in conjunction
with Snapdragon Editorial Group, Inc.
Associate Editor: Janice Jacobson
Design Manager: Amy J. Wenger
Design: The Office of Bill Chiaravalle

Printed in China
03 04 05/HK/ 4 3 2 1

The GIFT of ANGELS

INSPIRATIONAL ENCOUNTERS *with* GOD'S HEAVENLY MESSENGERS

inspirio™

TABLE OF CONTENTS

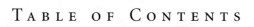

ANGELS SERVE AS GUARDIANS

The LORD will command his angels concerning you
to guard you in all your ways;
they will lift you up in their hands,
so that you will not strike your foot against a stone.

PSALM 91:11–12

The LORD said, "See, I am sending an angel ahead of you to guard you along the way and to bring you to the place I have prepared."

EXODUS 23:20

ANGELS SERVE AS GUARDIANS

SAFE FROM THE HAND OF HEROD

After Jesus was born in Bethlehem in Judea, during the time of King Herod, Magi from the east came to Jerusalem and asked, "Where is the one who has been born king of the Jews? We saw his star in the east and have come to worship him."

When King Herod heard this he was disturbed, and all Jerusalem with him. When he had called together all the people's chief priests and teachers of the law, he asked them where the Christ was to be born. "In Bethlehem in Judea," they replied, "for this is what the prophet has written . . . "

Then Herod called the Magi secretly and found out from them the exact time the star had appeared. He sent them to Bethlehem and said, "Go and make a careful search for the child. As soon as you find him, report to me, so that I too may go and worship him."

ANGELS SERVE
AS GUARDIANS

After they had heard the king, they went on their way, and the star they had seen in the east went ahead of them until it stopped over the place where the child was. When they saw the star, they were overjoyed. On coming to the house, they saw the child with his mother Mary, and they bowed down and worshiped him. Then they opened their treasures and presented him with gifts of gold and of incense and of myrrh. And having been warned in a dream not to go back to Herod, they returned to their country by another route.

When they had gone, an angel of the Lord appeared to Joseph in a dream. "Get up," he said, "take the child and his mother and escape to Egypt. Stay there until I tell you, for Herod is going to search for the child to kill him."

So he got up, took the child and his mother during the night and left for Egypt, where he stayed until the death of Herod. [1]

ANGELS SERVE
AS GUARDIANS

Everlasting God:
You have ordained and constituted—in a wonderful order—the ministries of
angels and mortals: Mercifully grant that, as your holy angels always serve and
worship you in heaven, so by your appointment they may help and defend us
here on earth; through Jesus Christ our Lord, who lives and reigns with you and
the Holy Spirit, one God, for ever and ever. Amen.

BOOK OF COMMON PRAYER

If you pray truly, you will feel within yourself a great assurance: and the angels
will be your companions.

EVAGRIUS OF PONTUS

Jacob also went on his way, and the angels of God met him. When Jacob saw
them, he said, "This is the camp of God!" So he named that place
Mahanaim.

GENESIS 32:1–2

Angels Serve as Guardians

Midnight Visitor

A young widow speaks of a time shortly after the death of her husband. Left to raise six children on her own, she depended heavily on family for support. With people around most of the day and plenty of work, she appeared brave. But after the children were all asleep in their beds and the house was quiet, fear would well up in her.

Each night she would lock the doors, and latch the windows, and turn on her bedside lamp to read. But she couldn't seem to conquer the fear and worry that crawled up under the quilt beside her. Everyday house noises amplified themselves. Every creak or rustling became a burglar with a weapon.

Reason flew out the window when fear settled in. Usually the young widow would read longer than she could afford to and then fall asleep with the lamp burning. No matter how she tried, she could not talk faith into her faltering heart.

ANGELS SERVE
AS GUARDIANS

"God," she prayed one night before finally dozing off, "I know I should not be fearful. I know the Bible says you will never forsake me, but I cannot see you. I cannot feel safe. Please, God, reassure me."

The widow awoke about midnight and lay, sensing that someone was in the room. There at the foot of the bed stood a tall man. He did not speak, and she did not speak. Oddly, she felt no fear at all. The widow stared at him, and he nodded slightly. She knew he was not really a man, but her very own guardian angel—the answer to her prayer.

She turned over and went back to sleep peacefully. Though she never saw the angel again, she knew he was there, watching over her and her children. Night time never again held her in a grip of fear and dread.[2]

ANGELS SERVE AS GUARDIANS

Dear Angel ever at my side,
How lovely you must be
To leave your home in heaven
To guard a one like me.

AUTHOR UNKNOWN

ANGELS SERVE
AS GUARDIANS

EVER WATCHFUL

One little phone call. That's all it took to turn Joan's world upside down. "Your test revealed some suspicious-looking cells. We'd like you to come back into the office today if possible." From there, the diagnosis was swift and devastating. Cancer. Within a few days, Joan was hospitalized for surgery.

In the hazy hours that followed the surgery, Joan slipped in and out of sleep, sometimes finding it difficult to distinguish between her dreams and the reality around her. But for a few moments on the second day, Joan struggled to be sure she was seeing what she thought she was seeing.

The man standing in the entryway of her room looked like her son, Chuck, but blinking to clear the haze, she realized she was mistaken. The pleasant looking stranger was dressed all in white. He did not come into the room to attend her, but simply stood leaning against the door facing. "His eyes never left mine. And my eyes did not leave his. His gaze was neither threatening nor

ANGELS SERVE
AS GUARDIANS

hospitable, but it was constant. I felt no fear of him but I was curious," she told her husband later. "I decided to ask who he was and why he was there."

Joan blinked to clear her vision one last time before speaking. But in that instant, the man had disappeared. She blinked again, hoping he would reappear. But it was to no avail—the man was gone.

Who was he? Joan believes with all her heart that God stationed an angel at the door of her room to watch over her as she recovered from the surgery, and for one brief minute, he allowed her to use her spiritual eyes to see him.

Joan recovered quickly from the surgery and the cancer has never returned.[3]

ANGELS SERVE
AS GUARDIANS

Hush! My dear; lie still and slumber;
Holy angels guard thy bed.
Heavenly blessings without number
Gently falling on thy head.

ISAAC WATTS

ANGELS SERVE
AS GUARDIANS

When the servant of the man of God got up and went out ...
an army with horses and chariots had surrounded the city.
"Oh, my lord, what shall we do?" the servant asked.

"Don't be afraid," the prophet answered. "Those who are
with us are more than those who are with them."

And Elisha prayed, "O LORD, open his eyes so he may see."
Then the LORD opened the servant's eyes, and he looked and saw
the hills full of horses and chariots of fire all around Elisha.

2 KINGS 6:15–17

ANGELS SERVE
AS GUARDIANS

An angel is a spiritual creature created by
God without a body, for the service
of Christendom and of the Church.

MARTIN LUTHER

ANGELS SERVE AS GUARDIANS

THROUGH THE STORM

Darcy was only ten the summer she and her parents visited Aunt Sally at her beach house on Ocracoke Island—part of North Carolina's Outer Banks. Though there were no other children for her to play with, Darcy had a wonderful time picking up shells on the beach and exploring her aunt's large and unusual home.

During their visit, Darcy had her own room on the second floor of the old house. Being an only child, she was used to sleeping alone, but the room was much bigger than her room at home. The windows were huge and the ceilings high. Darcy had a little trouble getting to sleep at night in her new surroundings.

That was especially true on the night a tropical storm blew in off the ocean. Late in the afternoon, the wind began to kick up the waves on the beach and by the time dinner was over, a driving rain was pounding down on the house. Through a process of clever distractions, Darcy managed to stay up with the adults much longer than usual. But finally, it was time.

ANGELS SERVE AS GUARDIANS

Her mother came upstairs with her, tucking her into bed and staying while she said her prayers. Darcy felt better. But once she was alone, she couldn't overcome what she felt when the flashes of lightning lit up the room and claps of thunder boomed just outside the oversized windows.

Finally, she could take it no longer. She threw back the covers, ran down the stairs, and into her father's arms.

"Why Darcy," her father said. "We're in no real danger. This old house has weathered many storms." Then he walked her back upstairs and tucked her in for a second time.

"Don't worry," her father said before leaving her bedside. "The Bible says that God has given his angels charge over us, to keep us in all our ways. You have nothing to fear. You go on to sleep now. I'll leave your door open and come up to check on you in a little bit."

ANGELS SERVE
AS GUARDIANS

After Darcy's father flipped off the light and went back downstairs, she lay awake in the darkness listening to the rain on the windows and counting between the lightning and thunder.

Just before dozing off, Darcy looked up to see a man standing in the doorway. In the dark room, she assumed it was her father making good on his promise.

Twice more during the stormy night, she awakened to see the shadowy figure looking in on her. Each time, she felt a deepening sense of peace and quickly went back to sleep.

When she awakened in the morning, bright sunshine filled the room, and she could see that the storm clouds had given way to clear blue sky. Darcy dressed quickly and went downstairs to join her mother, father, and Aunt Sally at the breakfast table.

"How did you sleep?" her mother asked.

Angels Serve as Guardians

"The storm woke me a few times," Darcy responded. "But each time, I saw Daddy looking in on me, and I wasn't afraid."

"That must have been your mother or your Aunt Sally," her father commented. "I meant to come up, but the storm caused some damage in the storeroom behind the kitchen. I got busy fixing that and just forgot."

"No, no," her mother responded. "It wasn't me. I thought your father was checking on you."

When everyone turned to Aunt Sally, she simply shook her head. "Must have been a guardian angel," she said, "watching over our Darcy girl!"[4]

ANGELS DELIVER US FROM HARM

The angel of the LORD encamps
around those who fear him,
and he delivers them.

PSALM 34:7

What's impossible to all humanity
may be possible to the metaphysics and physiology of angels.

JOSEPH GLANVILLE

ANGELS DELIVER
US FROM HARM

AN ANGEL DELIVERS PETER FROM PRISON

About this time, King Herod began to persecute some members of the church. He had James, the brother of John, put to death by the sword. When he saw that this pleased the Jews, he went ahead and had Peter arrested. (This happened during the time of the Festival of Unleavened Bread.) After his arrest Peter was put in jail, where he was handed over to be guarded by four groups of four soldiers each. Herod planned to put him on trial in public after Passover. So Peter was kept in jail, but the people of the church were praying earnestly to God for him.

The night before Herod was going to bring him out to the people, Peter was sleeping between two guards. He was tied with two chains, and there were guards on duty at the prison gate. Suddenly an angel of the Lord stood there, and a light shone in the cell.

The angel shook Peter by the shoulder, woke him up, and said, "Hurry! Get up!" At once the chains fell off of Peter's hands. Then the angel said,

ANGELS DELIVER
US FROM HARM

"Tighten your belt and put on your sandals." Peter did so, and the angel said, "Put your cloak around you and come with me."

Peter followed him out of the prison, not knowing, however, if what the angel was doing was real; he thought he was seeing a vision. They passed by the first guard station and then the second, and came at last to the iron gate that opened into the city. The gate opened for them by itself, and they went out. They walked down a street, and suddenly the angel left Peter.

Then Peter realized what had happened to him, and said, "Now I know that it is really true! The Lord sent his angel to rescue me from Herod's power and from everything the Jewish people expected to happen."

Aware of his situation, he went to the home of Mary, the mother of John Mark, where many people had gathered and were praying.[5]

ANGELS DELIVER US FROM HARM

Christians should never fail to sense the operation of angelic glory. It forever eclipses the world of demonic powers, as the sun does a candle's light.

BILLY GRAHAM

Our forefathers went down into Egypt, and we lived there many years. The Egyptians mistreated us and our fathers, but when we cried out to the LORD, he heard our cry and sent an angel and brought us out of Egypt.

NUMBERS 20:15–16

ANGELS DELIVER
US FROM HARM

The angels are the dispensers and administrators of the Divine beneficence toward us; they regard our safety, undertake our defense, direct our ways, and exercise a constant solicitude that no evil befall us.

JOHN CALVIN

In all the distress of [his people]
the LORD too was distressed,
and the angel of his presence saved them.
In his love and mercy he redeemed them;
he lifted them up and carried them
all the days of old.

ISAIAH 63:9

ANGELS DELIVER
US FROM HARM

RESCUER UNKNOWN

Huge drops of rain splattered the windshield. Soon Emily could no longer see to drive. Great flashes of lightning only blinded her even more. In desperation, she pulled over, turned on her emergency flashers and waited. The rain was deafening, but soon it let up, and she eased back unto the roadway.

It had been a tough finals week at the University. Emily was tired and anxious to get home. Then suddenly it happened. The steering wheel would not respond; the brakes were useless as she hydroplaned across the drenched pavement. She later remembered that she called out to God for help as the car careened off the highway, and everything went black.

Emily didn't remember the impact, but she did remember someone's strong arms lifting her out of the car. A reassuring voice urged her to "Rest. You're okay now."

She has no idea how long she laid there aware of raindrops falling softly on her face. Then suddenly, she saw flashing lights and heard sirens wailing. She

ANGELS DELIVER US FROM HARM

could smell something burning and quickly realized it was her car! Soon an ambulance driver knelt beside her, asking for her name and whether she had been alone in the car.

"Yes, I was alone in the car," she answered, "no passengers—only the man who pulled me out. Is he okay?"

"I'm the one who reported the accident," said a man standing nearby. "I did not see anyone else. When I came up, the car was already in flames, and this young woman was lying right where she is now."

"Maybe you got out by yourself," the paramedic suggested. But Emily knew that wasn't what had happened. She had heard a man's strong voice and felt him lifting her effortlessly, carrying her to safety. An angel? Emily thinks so.[6]

ANGELS DELIVER
US FROM HARM

*Jesus said, "Do you think I cannot call on my Father,
and he will at once put at my disposal
more than twelve legions of angels?"*

MATTHEW 26:53

*Angels are the undercover agents God
assigned to protect his children.*

BETSY WILLIAMS

*You are never alone.
Your guardian angel is right beside you always
ready to help at the slightest need.*

AUTHOR UNKNOWN

ANGELS DELIVER
US FROM HARM

FALLING OVER!

"An angel caught me, " Angela's thirteen-year-old son Nathaniel confided. "I've thought about it every way I can, and that's the only thing that makes sense."

The idea that God's angels are assigned to guard and protect us was not new to Nathaniel or his siblings, but with the advent of his preteen years, such truths had been greeted with a nervous giggle. "Right. Sure. Okay, Mom."

But it was clear that Nathaniel was now a believer, the result of an ill-advised climb out a second-story window and up to the top of the chimney to flush out a nest of starlings.

"I've got good news and bad news," he told Angela on the phone shortly after the "incident." She felt the instant panic and reluctance to ask for details that every working mother understands all too well.

ANGELS DELIVER
US FROM HARM

"And?" she finally asked weakly.

"The good news is those birds in the chimney are gone. The bad news is that I no longer have eyebrows or chest hair," he continued.

Before she could bring herself to ask for the whys and hows, Nathaniel explained that he had crouched over the chimney and poured in a "little" gasoline before striking a match and dropping it in. The ensuing fireball had blown him off the five-foot chimney and onto the steeply sloped roof.

Angela remembered rushing home that day—with a lengthy lecture on dangerous, foolhardy behavior, followed by a tag line on the imprudence of testing the Almighty screaming in her head. And she also remembered the joy she felt a few days later when her young son came to her with his interpretation of what had happened.[7]

ANGELS DELIVER
US FROM HARM

CAUGHT ON THE TRACKS

Marie and Anne had spent six wonderful weeks in Europe and were now capping off their trip with a visit to Marie's brother, who was on assignment in Naples. By the time the women reached the city, they thought of themselves as seasoned travelers. Their Euro rail passes were used up, but they felt confident enough to rent a car. Just in case, they practiced in a nearby neighborhood before navigating the streets. Their rented Fiat was slow but steady, and they felt they would do just fine.

Anne was driving, when the women suddenly found themselves caught in a maelstrom of honking cars. They were headed for the bay and could see the turquoise water off in the distance. But to get there, they would have to make several difficult maneuvers. First, they would have to cross two lanes of traffic, then enter an open steel door to cross two lanes of street car tracks, then exit through another open steel door, before getting onto the bay drive.

The women negotiated the traffic lanes without incident and made it through the first open steel door and onto the tracks. But then they were

ANGELS DELIVER
US FROM HARM

confronted by a terrible sound. WHRUMP! The car stopped on the tracks and both steel doors swung shut, locking them in! A street car was coming toward them, moving very fast. The last thing the women remember seeing was the terrified look of the streetcar driver. Then they closed their eyes and waited for the inevitable.

The women heard a gentle whoosh sound and then looked up to see that their car was now on the bay drive. Both steel doors were still closed and locked behind them. Through the partially open car window, Marie heard a pedestrian say to a companion, "Did you see what just happened? It's a miracle!"

Marie and Anne cannot explain what happened to them that day on the streets of Naples. All they can say for sure is that their confidence in themselves failed them, while their confidence in God and his mighty guardian angels was established for all time.[8]

ANGELS DELIVER
US FROM HARM

Angels, angels, so very strong
Obeying God's Word, even in song.
They are ready and alert for me.
Should I summon them on bended knee.

Angels, angels, flames of fire
Delivering God's message, awe to inspire
Doing His bidding whenever He calls
Subduing the enemy, giving us pause.

BETSY WILLIAMS[9]

ANGELS DELIVER US FROM HARM

I know that God is watching me
And sees the danger I can't see;
And in my very darkest hour
He sends his angels full of power
To guard me though I'm unaware
That they are even standing there.
God's angels guard me in life's way
And camp around me night and day.

ED STRAUSS [10]

ANGELS DELIVER
US FROM HARM

*Jesus said, "See that you do not look down on one
of these little ones. For I tell you that their angels
in heaven always see the face of my Father in heaven."*

MATTHEW 18:10

ANGELS DELIVER
US FROM HARM

FLAMING SWORDS

During the Mau Mau uprisings in East Africa in 1956, a band of roving Mau Maus came to the village of Lauri, surrounded it, and killed every inhabitant including the women and children—300 in all. No more than three miles away was the Rift Valley School, a private school where missionary children were being educated away from their missionary parents. Immediately upon leaving the carnage of Lauri, the Mau Maus came with spears, bows and arrows, clubs, and torches to the school with the same intentions of complete destruction.

Of course, you can imagine the fear of those little inhabitants along with their instructors housed in the boarding school. Word had already reached them about the destruction of Lauri—but there was no place to flee with little children and women. So the only resource was to go to prayer.

Angels Deliver
Us from Harm

Out of the darkness of the night, lighted torches were seen coming toward the school. Soon there was a complete ring of these terrorists about the school, cutting off all avenues of escape.

Shouting and curses could be heard coming from the Mau Maus. Then they began to advance on the school, tightening the circle, shouting louder, coming closer. But when they were finally close enough to throw a spear, they stopped !

The Mau Maus began to retreat and soon were running into the jungle.

A call had gone out to the authorities and an army had been sent in the direction of the school to rescue the inhabitants.

By the time the army arrived, the would-be assassins had dispersed. The army spread out in search of them and miraculously, captured the entire band of raiding Mau Maus.

ANGELS DELIVER US FROM HARM

Later, before the judge at their trial, the leader of the accused Mau Maus was called to the witness stand. "Did you kill the inhabitants at Lauri?" the judge asked.

"Yes," was the reply.

"Was it your intention to do the same at the missionary school in Rift Valley?" asked the judge.

"Yes," came the answer.

"Well then," asked the judge, "why didn't you attack the school?"

The leader of the accused Mau Maus answered, "We were on our way to attack and destroy all the people and school. But as we came closer, all of a sudden, between us and the school were many huge men, dressed in white with flaming swords. We became afraid and ran to hide!"[11]

ANGELS DELIVER
US FROM HARM

ANGEL BEHIND THE WHEEL

One sunny autumn afternoon, Karen left her home in northern Oklahoma and set out on a 550-mile road trip. She was only fifty miles from her destination when the unthinkable happened.

Approaching a red light in a city in northern Louisiana, Mary Alice suddenly heard the screeching and hissing of wheels behind her. Glancing up into the rearview mirror, she saw a truck bearing down on her, madly out of control.

It was too late to get out of the way, too late to do anything really, except brace herself and call out to the Lord for help. The crash was severe—dead center in the rear of her vehicle. The impact pushed her car perilously close to the car in front of her, which would have left her sandwiched between the two vehicles in a mass of twisted metal.

While sitting there in the car, fully conscious and miraculously unhurt, Mary Alice felt the presence of angels behind the wheels of her car—strong, comforting, and in control. They had come to her rescue at the very instant she had called out to the Lord for help.

ANGELS DELIVER
US FROM HARM

Mary Alice looked out the driver's window to see a shaken truck driver approaching. He opened the driver's door and helped her out, amazed at what he saw. Although her car was totaled, she did not have so much as a bruise.

"I'm so sorry," the truck driver said as sirens signaled that police and rescue workers were rushing to the scene. "I was sure we'd have to carry you out of here on a stretcher. You're a lucky woman," he continued.

"Not lucky—blessed!" Mary Alice insisted. "God's angels came to my rescue."[12]

The golden moments in the stream of life
rush past us and we see nothing but sand;
the angels come to visit us, and
we only know them when they are gone.

GEORGE ELLIOT

ANGELS DELIVER US FROM HARM

INCIDENT AT THE LAKE

Nanette was already an accomplished swimmer at the age of eleven. She practiced her strokes daily at a nearby lake. And that's where she was on a sunny August day—a day she almost did not survive.

She was proud of herself as she swam toward the raft near the center of the lake. Her stamina had increased significantly since the summer began. On that fateful day, she was able to swim out to the raft three times before becoming winded. She had decided to push herself to make one more trip out before quitting for the day. That's when she encountered Billy.

Nanette knew Billy—everyone did. His nickname was The Lakeside Bully, and he had earned the title fair and square.

As Nanette tried to swim around Billy, he grabbed her head and pushed her underwater. Even though she was already tired from swimming three laps to the raft, she was able to fight her way back up to the surface. Breaking through the water, Nanette gasped for air. She knew instantly that he was still there— waiting. Billy gritted his teeth and pushed her under again as far as he could.

Angels Deliver
Us from Harm

Nanette was now so tired that she felt she had no power to fight back. She felt like she was moving in slow motion. She remembers looking up and seeing the sun sparkling like diamonds through the dark green water. She knew she would never make it.

The next thing Nanette remembers was her head breaking through the surface of the water and a man leaning over the side of the raft reaching out to her. He pulled her onto the raft, asked if she was going to be all right, then dove in and swam for shore.

Nanette never did learn the identity of the man on the raft. As she swam her laps that morning, she had seen no one. Nor has she ever been able to explain how she made it to the surface and swam the rest of the way to the raft. Of that she has no memory at all. Nor can she say what happened to Billy. As she rested on the raft, he was nowhere in sight.

She may never completely understand the incident at the lake, but Nanette does have a theory. An angel pulled her from the dark, green waters. An angel sent from God.[13]

Angels Serve as Messengers

The word "angel" simply means "messenger."

Dan Schaeffer

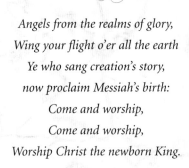

Angels from the realms of glory,
Wing your flight o'er all the earth
Ye who sang creation's story,
now proclaim Messiah's birth:
Come and worship,
Come and worship,
Worship Christ the newborn King.

JAMES MONTGOMERY

ANGELS SERVE AS MESSENGERS

THE BIRTH OF JESUS

In those days Caesar Augustus issued a decree that a census should be taken of the entire Roman world. (This was the first census that took place while Quirinius was governor of Syria.) And everyone went to his own town to register.

So Joseph also went up from the town of Nazareth in Galilee to Judea, to Bethlehem the town of David, because he belonged to the house and line of David. He west there to register with Mary, who was pledged to be married to him and was expecting a child. While they were there, the time came for the baby to be born, and she gave birth to her firstborn, a son. She wrapped him in cloths and placed him in a manger, because there was no room for them in the inn.

And there were shepherds living out in the fields nearby, keeping watch over their flocks at night. An angel of the Lord appeared to them, and the glory of the Lord shone around them, and they were terrified. But the angel said

Angels Serve
as Messengers

to them, "Do not be afraid. I bring you good news of great joy that will be for all the people. Today in the town of David a Savior has been born to you; he is Christ the Lord. This will be a sign to you: You will find a baby wrapped in cloths and lying in a manger."

Suddenly a great company of the heavenly host appeared with the angel, praising God and saying,

> *"Glory to God in the highest,*
> *And on earth peace to men on whom his favor rests."*

When the angels had left them and gone into heaven, the shepherds said to one another, "Let's go to Bethlehem and see this thing that has happened, which the Lord has told us about."

So they hurried off and found Mary and Joseph, and the baby, who was lying in the manger. When they had seen him, they spread the word concerning what had been told them about this child, and all who heard it were amazed at what the shepherds said to them. But Mary treasured up all these things

ANGELS SERVE
AS MESSENGERS

and pondered them in her heart. The shepherds returned, glorifying and praising God for all the things they had heard and seen, which were just as they had been told.[14]

It came upon the midnight clear,
That glorious song of old,
From Angels bending near the earth
To touch their harps of gold;
'Peace on the earth, good will to man
From Heaven's all gracious King.'
The world in solemn stillness lay
To hear the angels sing.

EDMUND HAMILTON SEARS

ANGELS SERVE AS MESSENGERS

ANGEL IN THE DOORWAY

Teresa had prayed for many years and long since given up hope. For whatever reason, it seemed that God had refused her request for a child.

She watched from her table in the restaurant as a couple fed their three children. The mother, ever vigilant, tended to their needs and reminded them to use their table manners. Teresa's heart ached at the sight.

In church, she watched from a seat in the sanctuary as a father comforted his little son during the long service. Her heart was warmed by the sight. Still, she was saddened that her own precious husband had no son to comfort.

Teresa heard every baby's cry and every toddler's lilting voice—constant reminders of what she had been denied.

The holidays were the most difficult. The stores seemed filled with children and stocked with children's things. Songs about Santa and the delights of the Christmas season bombarded her. She listened as friends talked of visits to

ANGELS SERVE
AS MESSENGERS

⎯⎯⎯⎯⎯ ∽ ⎯⎯⎯⎯⎯

grandma's house. The whole world vibrated with a sort of breathless expectation, except in her own small corner. There was no petite daughter for whom to buy a red velvet dress, no tow-headed boy for whom to place a toy train under the tree.

At every family gathering she faced the same, unanswerable question, "When are you two going to start a family?"

It was mid-December. Snow blanketed the town, and Teresa decided to go shopping. She chose a small tree from a corner lot strung with colored lights. Then she entered a dusty antique shop, where she found a darling tractor for her husband Jim's collection. The price tag almost stopped her, but with no children to buy gifts for she could swing it.

Heading across town, she stopped to the Sweet Shoppe to pick out some special goodies. Teresa was determined to make the best of things. She would go on home and bake some cookies to frost, put on some holiday music, and drink a cup of hot eggnog by the fire.

ANGELS SERVE
AS MESSENGERS

The cold had set in. She could feel the change. The temperature had dropped in the short time it took her to drive home.

The house sat dark when she pulled into the garage. How dreary to come home first and all alone to the empty rooms.

As she entered the kitchen from the garage, she felt a strangeness. Then she heard a bell and noticed a light as unobtrusive as a candle's glow in the room.

"Jim?" she called out. "Jim, are you home?"

No answer came back to her as she stepped into the dining room. There in the opposite doorway stood a bright personage, his white robe rippling around him as if blown by a strong wind.

Teresa knew instinctively that this person was no burglar, no housebreaker, and no danger to her. From across the room, she looked up at his face and was not afraid.

ANGELS SERVE
AS MESSENGERS

"I've come to bring you a message," he said. "Soon you will be given a child. Prepare your heart." Then he was gone.

The days passed quickly from winter into spring and then into summer. Autumn passed in a swirl of falling leaves and clouds of brown cowbirds.

In mid-December, the first snow fell blanketing the town. Teresa went shopping. At the corner lot, she bought the tallest tree. In the department store, she chose a red velvet dress. In the toy store, she bought a doll and a china tea set. Then across town, she went to the Sweet Shoppe. This Christmas, she and Jim had their own little daughter to dote on.[15]

ANGELS SERVE
AS MESSENGERS

God will deign to visit oft the dwellings of just men
Delighted, and with frequent intercourse
Thither will send his winged messengers
On errands of supernal grace.

JOHN MILTON

Around our pillows golden ladders rise,
And up and down the skies,
With winged sandals shod,
The angels come and go, the Messengers of God!

RICHARD HENRY STODDARD

Joseph had a dream in which he saw
a stairway resting on the earth, with its
top reaching to heaven, and the angels of God
were ascending and descending on it.

GENESIS 28:12

ANGELS SERVE AS MESSENGERS

THE SHINING STAFF

The walking stick he used was as tall as his shoulder, and covered with lumps as if it had been cut from an old, gnarled apple tree. It must have been wood. Parts of it were dark brown and others almost a light cream with all the shades of brown in between. At the top, where his big hand grasped it, it was wider and spindled down to a point. Somehow it shone with the translucence of an antique brown glass pharmacy bottle.

He wore a white robe that covered his feet and billowed around his sturdy legs as he walked purposefully forward. A cape of heavy gray woolen material curved around his shoulders, and the white sleeves of his robe showed from the elbows to the wrists of his wizened hands. His balding head was ringed with a circle of fuzzy gray hair. The skin of his scalp was bright red as if he had walked a long way in the hot sun.

It is Good Friday. He must be part of the company of a church play, Janie thought. Then she looked into his eyes. . .

ANGELS SERVE
AS MESSENGERS

Janie and her daughter Faith left home the week before Easter to visit friends in Oklahoma. It had been a last-minute trip—made in anger. Twenty-six years Janie had been married to Tom, and they had drifted further and further apart. Now they were merely housemates. They lived lives un-touching and un-loving, separate and desperately lonely.

Tom had gone off on a week-long hunting trip and left his wife and daughter to face yet another holiday alone.

Janie's friends in Oklahoma were happy to see the two—took them in, hugged and loved them. They sat in the spacious old house and talked while the children played. Little girls in high heels and dress-up gowns paraded down the staircase and across the bare wood floors. A small tow-headed boy drove his toy cars up and down the wooden lanes.

The weather was balmy for April so they sat on the swing out on the wide, airy front porch that evening. Happy, lilting voices spilled into the evening. These friends had a happy home, a happy marriage. The wife sat with bare

ANGELS SERVE
AS MESSENGERS

feet dangling as they talked and laughed, her long hair sweeping behind her, unaware of the pain Janie had hidden in the cold confines of her heart.

A young couple pulled up and the hostess called to them in welcome, "Have you had supper? There is soup and cornbread in the kitchen. Help yourselves." People seemed to flow in and out of that house. Happy voices, laughter, friends, love, music, children, peace, all the things Janie wanted that were missing from her life, she encountered there.

She lay in bed that night, awake. Wind sighed in the upper branches of a cottonwood tree outside the window. Sheer curtains blew into the room and fell still in the quiet.

"I can't go back, I can't! I won't! This is the way home and marriage and love should be. I can't go home." Janie struggled, tearfully fighting with her thoughts.

Soon the visit ended, and Janie and Faith loaded the car and said their goodbyes. With dread Janie drove back toward Mississippi. She wanted to drive

ANGELS SERVE AS MESSENGERS

off and never be found. She wanted to disappear from the face of the earth, yet, Faith needed her.

"Help me God," she prayed. "Help me go home."

The closer to Mississippi the car came, the more desperate Janie became. "I can't go back, I can't! God help me! Give me a sign."

That's when she saw him, a figure far off walking purposefully toward her. His white robe swirled around his legs, and his cloak curved in a wide half-circle from his broad shoulders. His bald head gleamed red in the noonday sun, as he came nearer and nearer. Janie slowed still more as the distance between them narrowed. He was such an odd sight—his staff luminescent.

When she finally reached him, Janie stopped the car and stared. The man stopped too and turned toward her car. He looked at her and spoke, though she isn't sure if he used real words or just impressions. In either case, the message was clear. "God knows. He knows where you've been and where

ANGELS SERVE
AS MESSENGERS

you're going. He knows what you're going through. Go home, now and trust him. He is with you every moment."

Janie turned to look at her daughter before driving on.

"Did you hear that, Faith?" Janie asked.

"Hear what?" she answered.

Janie turned back to the window, but the man was gone.

"Did you see the man with the staff?"

"What man, Mama?"[16]

ANGELS MINISTER TO OUR NEEDS

Are not all angels ministering
spirits sent to serve those who will
inherit salvation?

HEBREWS 1:14

Angelic beings are continually ministering to people in many ways in these present days. Many seeming coincidences are really angels on the job!

ROLAND BUCK

ANGELS MINISTER TO OUR NEEDS

THE ANGELS MINISTER TO ELIJAH

King Ahab told his wife Jezebel everything that Elijah had done and how he had put all the prophets of Baal to death. She sent a message to Elijah: "May the gods strike me dead if by this time tomorrow I don't do the same thing to you that you did to the prophets." Elijah was afraid and fled for his life; he took his servant and went to Beersheba in Judah.

Leaving the servant there, Elijah walked a whole day into the wilderness. He stopped and sat down in the shade of a tree and wished he would die. "It's too much, LORD," he prayed. "Take away my life; I might as well be dead!"

He lay down under the tree and fell asleep. Suddenly an angel touched him and said, "Wake up and eat." He looked around and saw a loaf of bread and a jar of water near his head. He ate and drank, and lay down again. The LORD's angel returned and woke him up a second time, saying, "Get up and eat, or the trip will be too much for you." Elijah got up, ate and drank, and the food gave him enough strength to walk forty days to Sinai, the holy mountain. There he went into a cave to spend the night.[17]

ANGELS MINISTER
TO OUR NEEDS

Remember to welcome strangers in your homes.
There were some who did that and
welcomed angels without knowing it.

HEBREWS 13:2 GNT

ANGELS MINISTER
TO OUR NEEDS

THE LAPEL PIN

The police detectives had packed up their equipment and left the scene of the robbery. They had taken down the bands of yellow ribbons that marked off the crime area. The glass countertops would have to be cleaned of the signs of fingerprinting dust. The store was quiet and the doors were locked.

David and Linda sat unspeaking and exhausted in the quiet. They had perked a pot of fresh coffee and taken their lunches from the refrigerator in the break room.

"We should eat." Linda said in an unconvincing voice. "It's two forty five, but my stomach is still churning. That gun looked so big!"

A rapping at the front door made them both jump. They looked at each other and moaned. The rap came again—gentle, polite, tap-tap-tap. Neither of them moved.

ANGELS MINISTER TO OUR NEEDS

David walked cautiously toward the front door. An old man smiled broadly and waved a hand in greeting.

"Can I help you?" David asked through the glass.

"I'd like to make a purchase. Your sign says you're open for business," chimed the gentleman in response.

David took the ring of shop keys and unlocked the door. Then he held it for the customer to enter. "I'm really sorry, Sir," David told the man. "We were just closing up. Our store was robbed today, and my wife and I are still a bit shaken up. If you need something right quick, I'll be willing to wait on you."

"I'm needing a watch fob," said the customer. "Have you got such a thing or has time passed me by?" I might like to look at a gold chain for a gift also."

The stranger was friendly and talkative. He took a while choosing the fob. Finally he selected one with a rough red ribbon and a gold clasp. None of the chains seemed to suit his fancy. "Could you order me one like I'm wanting?" he asked.

ANGELS MINISTER
TO OUR NEEDS

"Sure thing," David answered.

Linda stayed nearby. The stranger's voice was comforting, somehow calming to her shattered nerves. She watched him quietly and listened to his voice. She noted he wore a soft denim shirt and blue jeans. His shoes were brown, comfortable-looking loafers. His face had a relaxed, easy going fit to it. Wrinkles at the corners of his eyes spoke that he loved to laugh and nearly always smiled.

"I don't believe we have seen you around here before," she said.

"I'm only working here for a short time. Tell me about the robbery," he asked. "Was anyone hurt?"

"It was awful," confided Linda. "A man and a woman came in. She pulled out a gun, and he climbed right over the display case. I thought they were going to kill us. They took the men's rings—our most valuable stock and cleaned out our register. It will take us years to recoup."

"Police get them?" asked the broad-shouldered man.

ANGELS MINISTER TO OUR NEEDS

"Not yet," answered David. "That's why we were closing up. We're afraid they might come back."

"No," said the stranger. "They won't come back. The police will catch them, and your jewelry will be back in your store within the week."

"What a nutty thing for him to say," thought David as he rung up the sale.

"Nice pin," he remarked, nodding toward the lapel pin above the gentlemen's left shirt pocket. "Angels are big this year. I haven't come across that particular one though."

"Oh, yes, my pin. I'm a member of the angel society—an angel band, I like to say," he answered with a hearty laugh.

The man stayed all through that late afternoon, and they talked and laughed more and drank another pot of coffee. The visiting calmed the couple and reassured them of their ability to face the coming days.

ANGELS MINISTER
TO OUR NEEDS

When he finally said his goodbyes, David and Linda watched the man stride off confidently into the cool evening air. Turning back, they saw that he had left his watch fob lying on the countertop beside his empty coffee cup. And beside them lay a tiny silver angel lapel pin.

"Should you run after him?" cried Linda in dismay.

"No, he'll be back. He paid in advance for the gold chain, and it was a pricey one he chose. He'll be back to get them."

The chain David ordered came in two weeks later. Linda marked it sold and placed it in the showcase with the men's rings that the police had returned after the arrest of the robbers. The stranger never returned. The fob, the gold chain, and a tiny silver lapel pin are still there today.[18]

ANGELS MINISTER TO OUR NEEDS

UNWILLING ANGEL

It was winter, the kind Joy had never known before. The blizzard had blown into Michigan the week she and her family had arrived, and every day since had seen a new layer of snow.

Now Joy stood at an upstairs window watching the snowflakes. As she wiped a tear from the corner of her eye, she whispered a prayer, "Lord, I'm a southern girl. I'm used to sunshine."

She remembered the day her husband told her of his three-month assignment in Michigan in the middle of winter.

"Let's all go," he had said. "It will be an adventure!"

Now the adventure was fully underway, and Joy was feeling lonely. Her husband was working, and the children had joined others in the neighborhood building a snow fort in the park a block away. Joy gazed toward the park where every tree looked like a luminous Christmas tree, and the little pond glistened.

ANGELS MINISTER TO OUR NEEDS

Well, it's pretty. I can't say it isn't pretty, she whispered to herself.

Just then she saw the children. They were tumbling toward the house, in and out of snowdrifts. But who was that with them? Another boy?

"Hi, Mom! This is Buddy! I found him at the park!" her son called out.

For a moment, she could only stare. Buddy was surely the most un-kept child she had ever seen. He needed a hair cut. His jacket was stained. His wool cap was two sizes too big. His wet mittens were stuffed into his back pocket, and his hands were red. His nose was running.

As Joy closed the door behind the three of them, Buddy announced, "I been playin' with your boy at the park, so I come over here to see where you live!"

"I see. But does your mother know where you are?" Joy said a little too brusquely.

"Oh, she don't care none! She works nights and sleeps days. I don't have to be home until suppertime!" Buddy assured them all.

ANGELS MINISTER
TO OUR NEEDS

Suppertime? Good Grief! It's only 11 a.m.! Joy thought.

Joy served lunch on snack trays by the fire. When she put soup and cheese toast on Buddy's tray, he sat up straight. "Wowee! Thank you," he said heartily.

Out of the corner of her eye, she observed that Buddy's method of eating could best be described as "enthusiastic."

During the rest of the afternoon, the children romped throughout the house. At one point, Buddy stopped briefly and picked up a music book from the piano bench.

"I saw an organ once," he said. "It had long sticks under the bench that you push with your feet."

"That's right," Joy responded, barely glancing up from her magazine.

"I wish I could make an organ play," he said.

"I've often wished the same thing," she said softly.

ANGELS MINISTER TO OUR NEEDS

Buddy was quickly off again to play "sergeant" with a battalion of toy soldiers.

Now it was 4:00 p.m., and Joy was trying to think of ways to get rid of Buddy. What could she say? Surely there were chores to be done, homework waiting.

She made the suggestion as kindly as she could. They all agreed that they did have homework. "But before Buddy leaves, can we please have hot chocolate in front of the fire?" they begged.

Joy started to refuse, but it was such a simple request, and she knew it would warm Buddy for the long walk home.

Finally, the cups of hot chocolate were drained and the last of the marshmallows licked from the rims. Buddy started for the door, pulling on his stained jacket and the still damp mittens. What a relief, Joy thought. Suddenly, with his small hand on the doorknob, he turned to her son and said, "Say! Your mom's an angel!"

ANGELS MINISTER TO OUR NEEDS

Joy froze—the gracious compliment ringing in her ears. An angel? I, who so grudgingly gave him soup and cheese toast, who noticed his dirty shirt, but never once looked into his clear blue eyes? I, who deplored his mother's carelessness, and never wondered what circumstances would cause her to work through the long, weary night? she thought, rehearsing the day in her head.

How could I have been so insensitive, she wondered. I should have welcomed him. I should have given him more than a glance.

"O Dear Lord," Joy's heart whispered, "I've overlooked one of your little ones."

The door was open now, and her sudden tears felt cold on her cheeks. She bent down and put one arm around her son and the other around the ragamuffin. "Come back any time, Buddy," she said.

Buddy bounded down the steps and out into the snow. There he turned, and waved. His face was one big, beaming smile.

It was enough to give wings to an unwilling angel![19]

ANGELS MINISTER TO OUR NEEDS

MAILBOX ANGEL

The card came in the mail one simmering hot summer morning. No one expected it, least of all the Hollingworths.

Liz was good at making do. She'd been finding ways to get by for quite some time. But with each passing day, the challenge seemed to grow bigger. The problem was a precious baby boy born with a heart defect that required surgery shortly after his birth. He was recovering much to Liz and Rob's great joy, but the medical bills continued to flood in. It seemed like each day some doctor or service had to be added to the pile.

Liz and Rob struggled to keep the mortgage paid, nutritious food on the table, and the utilities paid. They managed without new shoes and clothes. And the food budget was stretched with beans and rice. The couple and their older children tilled up most of the backyard and planted a garden of peas, tomatoes and squash to help the family through the spare days. Still the family barely got by.

ANGELS MINISTER
TO OUR NEEDS

The card came early one afternoon. Liz sat down on the porch steps and looked at it for a while. She never hurried to open mail. Most of it was bills anyway. But this card seemed different. The address was hand written and there was no return address—only a postmark that read Depew, Oklahoma. The town was about an hour away. Who did she know there? No one. Not one single person.

Liz opened the envelope, unsealing the gold fish symbol on the back flap, and marveled at what she saw. The front of the card featured an angel in flight—a rather Americanized angel in a patchwork gown with quilted wings. A pair of sandals graced her feet and a tin ring of a halo attempted unsuccessfully to hold her hair down. Blond wisps of hair curled and streamed back behind her in the wind. Inside, Liz found a short poem—a couplet: "For buttons and bows and shoes for your toes," accompanied by gift certificates to a Wal-Mart store. Each $50.00 certificate was addressed to one of the children with a larger amount for Liz and her husband. The certificates were signed "Your Guardian Angel."

ANGELS MINISTER TO OUR NEEDS

Liz held the card to her heart and cried for joy. She knew the hospital bills would continue to pile up on the desk inside. But something had changed inside her heart. She felt this gift was a down-payment of sorts. In his way, in his time, God would minister to all their needs.[20]

In this dim world of clouding cares,
We rarely know, till 'wildered eyes
See white wings lessening up the skies,
The angels with us unawares.

GERALD MASSEYH

ANGELS TELL US
ABOUT THE FUTURE

Angels mean messengers and ministers.
Their function is to execute the plan
of divine providence, even in earthly things.

SAINT THOMAS AQUINAS

Angels are spirits, but it is not because they are spirits that
they are angels. They become angels when they are sent.
For the name angel refers to their office, not their nature.
You ask the name of this nature, it is spirit; you ask its office,
it is that of an Angel, which is a messenger.

SAINT AUGUSTINE

ANGELS TELL US
ABOUT THE FUTURE

DANIEL'S VISION

In the third year that Cyrus was emperor of Persia, a message was revealed to Daniel, who is also called Belteshazzar. The message was true but extremely hard to understand. It was explained to him in a vision.

At that time I was mourning for three weeks. I did not eat any rich food or any meat, drink any wine, or comb my hair until the three weeks were past.

On the twenty-fourth day of the first month of the year I was standing on the bank of the mighty Tigris River. I looked up and saw someone who was wearing linen clothes and a belt of fine gold. His body shone like a jewel. His face was as bright as a flash of lightning, and his eyes blazed like fire. His arms and legs shone like polished bronze, and his voice sounded like the roar of a great crowd.

I was the only one who saw the vision. Those who were with me were terrified and ran and hid. I was left there alone, watching this amazing vision. I had no strength left, and my face was so changed that no one could have recognized

ANGELS TELL US
ABOUT THE FUTURE

me. When I heard his voice, I fell to the ground unconscious and lay there face downward. Then a hand took hold of me and raised me to my hands and knees; I was still trembling.

The angel said to me, "Daniel, God loves you. Stand up and listen carefully to what I am going to say. I have been sent to you." When he had said this, I stood up, still trembling.

Then he said, "Daniel, don't be afraid. God has heard your prayers ever since the first day you decided to humble yourself in order to gain understanding. I have come in answer to your prayer. The angel prince of the kingdom of Persia opposed me for twenty-one days. Then Michael, one of the chief angels, came to help me, because I had been left there alone in Persia. I have come to make you understand what will happen to your people in the future. This is a vision about the future."[21]

Angels Tell Us
about the Future

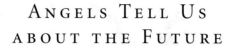

*John the Apostle wrote, " Then I saw another
angel flying high in the air, with an eternal message of
Good News to announce to the peoples of the earth, to every
race, tribe, language, and nation. He said in a loud voice,
"Honor God and praise his greatness! For the time has come
for him to judge all people. Worship him who made heaven,
earth, sea, and the springs of water!"*

REVELATION 14:6−7 GNT

Angels Tell Us about the Future

An Angel Tells Paul What Will Happen

After the men had gone a long time without food, Paul stood up before them and said: "Men, you should have taken my advice not to sail from Crete; then you would have spared yourselves this damage and loss. But now I urge you to keep up your courage, because not one of you will be lost; only the ship will be destroyed. Last night an angel of the God whose I am and whom I serve stood beside me and said, 'Do not be afraid, Paul. You must stand trial before Caesar; and God has graciously given you the lives of all who sail with you.' So keep up your courage, men, for I have faith in God that it will happen just as he told me.[22]

ANGELS TELL US
ABOUT THE FUTURE

WORDS OF RECONCILIATION

Michele was roused out of a deep sleep by the sense of someone standing over her. What she saw was an incredible sight, a radiant angel at the side of her bed.

He didn't say, "Don't be afraid," but all the same she felt no fear. His voice was deep and as warm as the sun. "You need to know your father is dying," the angel said.

He lingered a moment, as if to give Michele time to consider his words. Then he drew back and was gone.

Michele hadn't seen her mother in the last year and hadn't seen much of her father. Her mother had trouble accepting Michele's husband and would never attend family events that included his parents or siblings. Things had come to a bitter stand off.

Pondering the message the angel had brought her, Michele wondered what God wanted her to do now. For years, any gesture of kinship she made turned futile – finally she had given up. Did God mean for her to reach out

ANGELS TELL US
ABOUT THE FUTURE

again? Why would her efforts be received differently now? She wondered if her parents even knew of her father's dire situation.

With Christmas just around the corner, Michele decided to invite her parents to the family celebration that would be held in her home, scarcely expecting them to come. To her surprise—and joy—they did. Suddenly, barriers that had separated the family for so long seemed to be coming down. A bridge to reconciliation was being forged.

A few weeks later, Michele's mother called to tell her that her father was sick. A doctor's visit in February brought the diagnosis—lung cancer.

Michele was thankful that she had acted on the angel's message from God to her. She knew that, soon, her mother would need help to care for her father, and now she could offer help.

Michele's father died in June that year. With the care of his family, he was able to spend those last months at home, as he wished, instead of in a hospital.

Michele will always cherish those days—gifts really—given to her by the Lord, through the words of an angel.[23]

ANGELS TELL US
ABOUT THE FUTURE

The Scripture says there is a time to be born and a time to die.
And when my time to die comes, an angel will be there to comfort me.
He will give me peace and joy even at that most critical hour and
usher me into the presence of God, and I will dwell with the
Lord forever. Thank God for the ministry of his blessed angels.

BILLY GRAHAM

ANGELS
WORSHIP GOD

Praise the L<small>ORD</small>, you his angels,
you mighty ones who do his bidding,
who obey his word.

P S A L M   1 0 3 : 2 0

We praise thee, O God: we acknowledge
thee to be the Lord.
All the earth doth worship thee:
the Father everlasting.
To thee all Angels cry aloud: the Heavens,
and all the Powers therein.
To thee Cherubin, and Seraphin: continually do cry,
Holy, Holy, Holy: Lord God of Sabaoth;
Heaven and earth are full of the Majesty:
of thy Glory.

MORNING PRAYER TE DEUM

ANGELS WORSHIP GOD

ANGELS SURROUND THE THRONE OF GOD

I [the Apostle John] saw an open door in heaven.

And the voice that sounded like a trumpet, which I had heard speaking to me before, said, "Come up here, and I will show you what must happen after this." At once the Spirit took control of me. There in heaven was a throne with someone sitting on it. His face gleamed like such precious stones as jasper and carnelian, and all around the throne there was a rainbow the color of an emerald. In a circle around the throne were twenty-four other thrones, on which were seated twenty-four elders dressed in white and wearing crowns of gold. ... In front of the throne seven lighted torches were burning, which are the seven spirits of God. Also in front of the throne there was what looked like a sea of glass, clear as crystal.

Surrounding the throne on each of its sides, were four living creatures covered with eyes in front and behind. The first one looked like a lion; the second looked like a bull; the third had a face like a human face; and the fourth

ANGELS WORSHIP GOD

looked like an eagle in flight. Each one of the four living creatures had six wings, and they were covered with eyes, inside and out. Day and night they never stop singing:

"Holy, holy, holy, is the Lord God Almighty,
who was, who is, and who is to come."

The four living creatures sing songs of glory and honor and thanks to the one who sits on the throne, who lives forever and ever. When they do so, the twenty-four elders fall down before the one who sits on the throne, and worship him who lives forever and ever. They throw their crowns down in front of the throne and say,

"Our Lord and God! You are worthy
to receive glory, honor, and power.
For you created all things,
and by your will they were given existence
and life."[24]

ANGELS
WORSHIP GOD

Angels, help us to adore Him;
Ye behold Him face to face.
Sun and moon, bow down before Him,
Dwellers all in time and space.
Praise Him! Praise Him!
Praise with us the God of grace.

HENRY FRANCIS LYTE

ANGELS WORSHIP GOD

Praise the LORD *from the heavens,*
praise him in the heights above.
Praise him, all his angels,
praise him, all his heavenly hosts.

PSALM 148:1-2

ANGELS
WORSHIP GOD

THE TABERNACLE OF GOD

Sheila was basically a homebody. She had traveled very little and never out of the United States. That's why signing up for a trip to Mexico to help a small congregation build a church was such a big step of faith.

"I won't kid you," Pastor Burkhardt told her. "It's a lot of hard work. We put in long days, pouring cement, laying brick, but every minute is worth it. The people are so kind and good. It's a pleasure to help them. A trip like this can change you forever." Pastor's words and her friends who had been on previous trips finally convinced Sheila to step out in faith and try something new.

Sheila tried many times to imagine what the small village would look like. But when the bus finally pulled up, she couldn't believe it. The main street was muddy from recent rains. She saw no traffic signals and only a few mud-spattered cars. Even though it was only thirty miles from Juarez, the city where the church group was staying, the little village had none of the big city's civilized amenities. The people lived in stark poverty. Their homes

ANGELS
WORSHIP GOD

were made of mud and tin and anything else they could find. There was no plumbing.

"Where do the people worship now?" she asked someone from her group.

"They meet here in the street," was the answer.

Pastor Burkhardt was right. The days were long and the work was hard. Each day for two weeks, they drove over terrible roads to the little village. Finally, a small, single room, concrete building sat at the end of the main street.

Working with the villagers had been an unexpected blessing for Sheila. Even though they spoke little English and she spoke no Spanish, she could see that they were kind and gracious people. More than once, one of the villagers had taken her hand and quietly prayed for her as she worked.

Even at that, Sheila's greatest blessing was yet to come. On their last day in the small town, a service was held in the new church. A few chairs were distributed about the room, but most sat on blankets on the floor. The villagers sang with fervor and spent much time in enthusiastic prayer. Sheila sat

ANGELS
WORSHIP GOD

quietly observing. The church they seemed so grateful to have was nothing like the beautiful, spacious church she was used to at home with its soft pews and carpeted floors.

"How can they be satisfied with so little?," she whispered to the Lord. Just then she looked up and could not believe what she was seeing. Two angels stood, with wings outspread in the front of the church just behind the altar. Two more stood in the back.

Sheila only saw the angels for a few moments, but she sensed their presence throughout the service. And she knew that God had given her the answer to her question. Who could ask for more than the privilege of worshipping God in the presence of his holy angels? It transformed even the crude building into the Sanctuary of God.[25]

Angels Worship God

Ye holy angels bright,
Who wait at God's right hand,
Or through the realms of light
Fly at your Lord's command,
Assist our song,
Or else the theme
Too high doth seem
For mortal tongue.

John Hampden Gurney

ANGELS
WORSHIP GOD

All the angels were standing around the throne and
around the elders and the four living creatures.
They fell down on their faces before the throne and worshiped God,
saying: "Amen! Praise and glory and wisdom and thanks and honor and
power and strength be to our God for ever and ever.
Amen!"

REVELATION 7:11-12

Angels Carry Out
the Purposes of God

— ∽∽ —

In speaking of the angels, God says,
"He makes his angels winds, and
his servants flames of fire."

Hebrews 1:7

— ∽∽ —

Angels take different forms at the bidding of their master,
God, and thus reveal themselves to men and
unveil the divine mysteries to them.

SAINT JOHN OF DAMASCUS

ANGELS CARRY OUT THE PURPOSES OF GOD

ANGELS PERFORM THEIR DUTIES

I [the Apostle John] saw four angels standing at the four corners of the earth, holding back the four winds so that no wind should blow on the earth or the sea or against any tree. And I saw another angel coming up from the east with the seal of the living God. He called out in a loud voice to the four angels to whom God had given the power to damage the earth and the sea. The angel said, "Do not harm the earth, the sea, or the trees, until we mark the servants of our God with a seal on their foreheads." And I was told that the number of those who were marked with God's seal on their foreheads were 144,000. They were from the twelve tribes of Israel, twelve thousand from each tribe: Judah, Reuben, Gad, Asher, Naphtali, Manasseh, Simeon, Levi, Issachar, Zebulun, Joseph, and Benjamin.

When the Lamb broke open the seventh seal, there was silence in heaven for about half an hour. Then I saw the seven angels who stand before God, and they were given seven trumpets.

ANGELS CARRY OUT THE PURPOSES OF GOD

Another angel, who had a gold incense container, came and stood at the altar. He was given a lot of incense to add to the prayers of all God's people and to offer it on the gold altar that stands before the throne. The smoke of the burning incense went up with the prayers of God's people from the hands of the angel standing before God. Then the angel took the incense container, filled it with fire from the altar, and threw it on the earth. There were rumblings and peals of thunder, flashes of lightning, and an earthquake.

Then the seven angels with the seven trumpets prepared to blow them.[26]

Praise the Lord, all you heavenly powers,
you servants of his, who do his will!

PSALM 103:21 GNT

ANGELS CARRY OUT THE PURPOSES OF GOD

There are two angels; that attend unseen
Each one of us, and in great books record
Our good and evil deeds. He who writes down
The good ones, after every action closes
His volume, and ascends with it to God.
The other keeps his dreadful day-book open
Till sunset, that we may repent; which doing,
The record of the action fades away,
And leaves a line of white across the page.

HENRY WADSWORTH LONGFELLOW

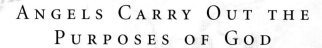

ANGELS CARRY OUT THE PURPOSES OF GOD

THE HITCHHIKER

Reverend Dwyan Calvert felt exhilarated as he climbed into his blue Nova and started down the highway. Along with a number of other ministers from the area, he had spent the last twenty-seven hours in prayer.

Together the men had poured out their hearts, interceded for the people of the area in general and their own congregations in particular, and worshipped God with great enthusiasm. Now it was 2:30 a.m., and Reverend Calvert was just now leaving Lubbock on his way back to Muleshoe, Texas. There were thirty-five miles of dark, moonless, west Texas highway between him and home. But Dwyan didn't care. He was happy to spend the time singing and praising God.

The first half of the ride to Muleshoe was uneventful, the highway deserted, the night still. Whether it was the darkness or his own reverie, Dwyan did not notice the car pulled over on the shoulder until it was only a few yards ahead. He slowed down and saw that two men were working on the car's passenger side, perhaps changing a tire.

ANGELS CARRY OUT THE PURPOSES OF GOD

Dwyan thought about stopping, but quickly discarded the idea. After all, the men seemed to be working on the problem, and no one would argue that it could be dangerous to stop to help strangers on a deserted highway in the middle of the night.

On down the road, Dwyan tried to return to his happy disposition and songs of praise, but instead of jubilation, he was feeling a tug at his heart. Wouldn't anyone be reluctant to stop at this hour? He asked himself again. But the unsettling inner tug would not go away.

"Lord," he prayed, trying to find his way back to his exuberant former self, "you know that could have been a dangerous situation. Who knows what those people were up to? Besides, it's too late to turn back. I'm sure they will all be fine."

With that, Dwyan started singing his favorite worship song, but didn't feel any better. Finally, in desperation, he prayed, "Lord, I see now that I should have opened my heart to those people. They needed my help, and I drove

ANGELS CARRY OUT THE PURPOSES OF GOD

right past. I give you my word that will not happen again. No matter how dark and how late, the next time I see someone who needs my help, I'll stop."

The words had barely passed his lips, when a man stepped from the darkness and waved. Dwyan saw no car on the shoulder, no house nearby. Nevertheless, he quickly stopped the car and backed to where the stranger was standing.

The man made his way quickly to the passenger door and hopped in without being formally asked.

"Hi, I'm Reverend Calvert," Dwyan said, offering his hand.

"Hello to you," the man responded. "I've been expecting you."

"Where are you headed?" Dwyan asked, puzzling over the man's strange reply.

"Just up here a ways," the man answered.

ANGELS CARRY OUT THE PURPOSES OF GOD

The two rode along quietly for a few miles before the man asked, "Where have you been tonight?"

"A prayer meeting," Dwyan responded.

The man nodded in a friendly manner, but said nothing.

When they reached the town of Sudan, Texas, the stranger told Dwyan that he could let him out near the square of the little town. When Dwyan dropped him off, the man shook his hand and thanked him for stopping.

Dwyan could see the man standing under the streetlight as he drove back onto the highway. He'd already gotten the point. God had sent an angel to remind him that serving him was more than high-minded words and spiritual activities. Serving God means reaching out beyond your fears, beyond your convenience, beyond your own personal agenda. It means actions as well as words. Reverend Calvert spent the rest of the trip worshipping God quietly and asking for a humble, tender heart toward the world around him.[27]

ANGELS CARRY OUT THE PURPOSES OF GOD

PUNCHED BY AN ANGEL

Mark was home from college, working as an installer for a garage door company and enjoying the comfortable warmth of a southern California summer. He liked the work, liked his co-workers, and liked taking a break from his studies to do some physical work.

On the day in question, Mark and a co-worker were installing a large garage door at a Honda dealership. The two of them carefully positioned the door, checking and double-checking to see that the tension chains were in place. The dealership employees stopped to watch as the two men began to crank the 500-pound door up above their heads. With Mark on one end and his co-worker on the other, they carefully wound the chain around the spring, testing for the right amount of tension.

They had performed this task many times before, but today was to be different. An unnoticed area of rotten wood above the door opening gave way at the worst possible moment. Mark looked up to see the door literally falling

ANGELS CARRY OUT THE PURPOSES OF GOD

on his head. The next thing he knew, the door crashed to the concrete and he was slammed up against the side wall a few feet away.

Those standing nearby rushed to his side. They were relieved to find that he was okay, just shaken and windless.

All the observers agreed on several facts. They had heard a loud pop as the cable holding the door in place broke. For a split second, everything seemed to be suspended in mid-air. Then they saw Mark fly backward toward the wall as though he had been punched in the chest.

That night in the shower, Mark noticed a grapefruit-size bruise on his chest. Checking it out in the mirror, he could clearly see knuckle marks. Had an angel punched him in the chest in order to keep him from being injured by the falling door? Did God have a special purpose for Mark's life? Had an angel been given the responsibility to see that Mark lived to accomplish that purpose?

Mark found these questions even more compelling when he awoke in the morning to discover that the dark purple bruise was completely gone![28]

ANGELS CARRY OUT THE PURPOSES OF GOD

God will send his angels with a loud trumpet call,
and they will gather his elect from the four winds,
from one end of the heavens to the other.

MATTHEW 24:31

ANGELS CARRY OUT THE PURPOSES OF GOD

THE WATCHMEN

In spite of the dangers, Von Asselt and his wife sensed a call to take up missionary work among wild Battas tribe in Sumatra. "The first two years," Von Asselt said, "were such that I shudder as I think about them. Frequently it seemed as if we were encompassed not only by hostile men but by hostile powers of darkness."

One day a Batta leader came to the missionary and said, "Now Tuan (which means teacher) I have one request. I would like to see your watchmen."

"What watchmen?" he asked in astonishment. "I have no watchmen!"

"The watchmen you station around your house at night to protect you," the visitor said.

"But I have no watchmen," he repeated. "I have only a little herdsboy and a little cook, and they would make poor watchmen."

The man looked incredulous, and said "Do not make me believe otherwise for I know better. May I look through your house to see if they are hidden there?"

ANGELS CARRY OUT THE PURPOSES OF GOD

"Certainly," the missionary replied, laughing, "Look through my house, but you will not find anyone." So the leader went in and searched every corner, even going through the beds. At last, he came out very much disappointed.

"When you first came here," he said, "we were very angry with you. So we resolved to kill you and your wife. We went to your house night after night, but when we came near there always stood close around the house, shoulder to shoulder, a double row of watchmen armed with glistening weapons. We dared not attack them to get into the house.

"We were, however, unwilling to abandon our plan so we went to a professional assassin. We asked him if he would kill you and your wife, telling him who you were, and of the watchmen we had seen protecting your house. He laughed at us and said, 'I fear no God and no devil and will get through those watchmen easily.'

"So we all came together in the evening and the assassin, swinging his weapon about his head, went courageously on before us. As we neared your house we remained in the background and let him go on alone. In a short

ANGELS CARRY OUT THE PURPOSES OF GOD

time, he came running back and said, 'No, I dare not risk going through alone. Two rows of big, strong men are there, very close together, and their weapons shine like fire.' So we gave up the thought of killing you. But tell me, Tuan, who are those watchmen? Have you ever seen them?"

"No," the missionary replied, "I have never seen them."

"And your wife, has she ever seen them?" he asked.

"No," the missionary answered, "my wife has never seen them. But I am not surprised to hear your story."

The missionary went into his house and brought out a Bible. Opening it, he said to the Batta leader, "This Book is the Word of our great God. In it, he has given this promise." Then he began to read: "The Angel of the Lord encamps around about those who fear him, and he delivers them" (Psalm 34:7)."

"You see," the missionary said, "we firmly believe in our God and that his promises are true. Therefore we do not need to see the watchmen. But you do not believe. Therefore our God had to show you the watchmen that you might learn to believe."[29]

THE ANGEL
OF THE LORD

*The angel of the L*ORD *encamps around those who fear him,*
and he delivers them.

PSALM 34:7

In Scripture we uniformly read that angels are heavenly spirits,
whose obedience and ministry God employs to execute all the purposes.
which he has decreed, and hence their name as being a kind
of intermediate messenger to manifest his will to men.

JOHN CALVIN

THE ANGEL
OF THE LORD

THE ANGEL OF THE LORD VISITS GIDEON

The angel of the LORD came and sat down under the oak in Ophrah that belonged to Joash the Abiezrite, where his son Gideon was threshing wheat in a winepress to keep it from the Midianites. When the angel of the LORD appeared to Gideon, he said, "The LORD is with you, mighty warrior."

"But sir," Gideon replied, "if the LORD is with us, why has all this happened to us? Where are all his wonders that our fathers told us about when they said, 'Did not the LORD bring us up out of Egypt?' But now the LORD has abandoned us and put us into the hand of Midian."

The LORD turned to him and said, "Go in the strength you have and save Israel out of Midian's hand. Am I not sending you?"

"But Lord," Gideon asked, "how can I save Israel? My clan is the weakest in Manasseh, and I am the least in my family."

The Angel
of the Lord

The Lord answered, "I will be with you, and you will strike down all the Midianites together."

Gideon replied, "If now I have found favor in your eyes, give me a sign that it is really you talking to me. Please do not go away until I come back and bring my offering and set it before you."

And the Lord said, "I will wait until you return."

Gideon went in, prepared a young goat, and from an ephah of flour he made bread without yeast. Putting the meat in a basket and its broth in a pot, he brought them out and offered them to him under the oak.

The angel of God said to him, "Take the meat and the unleavened bread, place them on this rock, and pour out the broth." And Gideon did so. With the tip of the staff that was in his hand, the angel of the Lord touched the meat and the unleavened bread. Fire flared from the rock, consuming the meat and the bread. And the angel of the Lord disappeared. When Gideon

THE ANGEL
OF THE LORD

realized that it was the angel of the LORD, he exclaimed, "Ah, Sovereign LORD! I have seen the angel of the Lord face to face!"

But the Lord said to him, "Peace! Do not be afraid. You are not going to die."

So Gideon built an altar to the Lord there and called it The Lord is Peace. To this day it stands in Ophrah of the Abiezrites.[30]

Christians should never fail to sense the operation
of an angelic glory. It forever eclipses the world of demonic powers,
as the sun does a candle's light.

BILLY GRAHAM

THE ANGEL
OF THE LORD

Angels are the chosen ambassadors of God
Announcing his coming
Just as the buglers go before
Announcing the arrival of the king.

ANDREA GARNEY

"I, Jesus, have sent my angel to give you this
testimony for the churches, I am the Root
and the Offspring of David, and the bright Morning star."

REVELATION 22:16

126

ACKNOWLEDGEMENTS

1. *Safe from the Hand of Herod*, Matthew 2:1–5, 7–15.
2. *Midnight Visitor*, interview and writing by Elece Hollis, Morris, Oklahoma.
3. *Ever Watchful*, Joan Steele, Tulsa, Oklahoma.
4. *Through the Storm*, interview and writing by Rebecca Currington, Tulsa, Oklahoma.
5. *An Angel Delivers Peter from Prison*, Acts 12:1–12 GNT.
6. *Rescuer Unknown*, interview and writing by Elece Hollis, Morris, Oklahoma.
7. *Falling Down*, interview and writing by Rebecca Currington, Tulsa, Oklahoma.
8. *Caught on the Tracks,* Marie Asner, Overland Park, Kansas.
9. Poem by Betsy Williams, used by permission.
10. Poem by Ed Strauss, used by permission.
11. *Flaming Swords*, Morris Plotts, New Sharon Assembly of God, New Sharon, Iowa. Used by permission.
12. *Angel Behind the Wheel*, Mary Alice Trent, Tulsa, Oklahoma.
13. *Incident at the Lake*, Nanette Thorsen-Snipes, Buford, Georgia.
14. *The Birth of Jesus,* Luke 2:1–15
15. *Angel in the Doorway*, interview and writing by Elece Hollis, Morris, Oklahoma.
16. *The Shining Staff*, interview and writing by Elece Hollis, Morris, Oklahoma.
17. *The Angels Minister to Elijah,* 1 Kings 19:1–9 GNT.
18. *The Lapel Pin*, interview and writing by Elece Hollis, Morris, Oklahoma.
19. *Unwilling Angel*, Joy Morgan Davis, Dallas, Texas
20. *Mailbox Angel*, interview and writing by Elece Hollis, Morris, Oklahoma
21. *Daniel's Vision*, Daniel 10:1–14 GNT
22. *An Angel Tells Paul What Will Happen*, Acts 27:21–25
23. *Words of Reconciliation,* Michele Marr, Huntington Beach, California
24. Angels Surround the Throne of God, Revelation 4:1–11 GNT
25. *The Tabernacle of God,* interview and writing by Rebecca Currington, Tulsa, Oklahoma
26. *Angels Perform Their Duties,* Revelation 7:1–8; 8:1–6 GNT
27. *The Hitchhiker*, Reverend Dwyan Calvert, Lufkin, Texas
28. *Punched by an Angel*, Mark Moesta, Tulsa, Oklahoma
29. *The Watchmen,* Dick Innes, ACTS International, Arcadia, California
30. *The Angel of the Lord Visits Gideon*, Judges 6:11–24

At Inspirio we love to hear from you—your stories, your feedback, and your product ideas.
Please send your comments to us
by way of e-mail at
icares@zondervan.com
or to the address below:

inspirio

Attn: Inspirio Cares
5300 Patterson Avenue SE
Grand Rapids, MI 49530

If you would like further information
about Inspirio and the products we
create please visit us at:
www.inspiriogifts.com

Thank you and God Bless!